CAN I _PLEASE_ RETIRE NOW?

A NURSE'S TRUE STORY

Written by Suzanne A. Ries R. N., M.S. N.

Designed, formatted and edited by
Kathryn Long
Cover illustration by Laura Sammartino

First Edition, published by Amazon KDP
July 2023
Copyright SAR-KL-07-26-23

copyright
l rights reserve

TABLE OF CONTENTS

INTRODUCTION

This book is a labor of love, written to serve a dual purpose. My main reason is to address a growing problem in the medical industry, including nursing. The second purpose is cathartic. I found myself traumatized by my personal experiences, which I can only describe as open and bleeding wounds. These experiences included threats of and actual physical violence, verbal and emotional abuse by coworkers, patients, and, worst of all, by nurse teachers and supervisors, existing in an ancient profession Florence Nightingale started in 1851 to serve mankind.

I recently spoke with a therapist in Australia. She is an ICU nurse turned therapist, specializing in helping nurses who have been traumatized by various experiences like mine on their jobs or during training. Speaking with her helped me see this is a far more universal problem than I first realized. It helped me to know these things were not personal only to me, but happen to nurses the world over. I hope my book will help other nurses to understand they are not alone.

The world recently went through a troubled time with the Covid-19 pandemic, where the medical profession, especially doctors and nurses, carried a heavy load. They showed courage and dedication and effectively drew a rainbow of hope through the darker seedier side of medicine. I hope everyone who reads this book will not just stop with being horrified over the true events revealed here but will also pray for and lobby for genuine changes that will leave the medical profession, and nursing in particular, in a more healthy and effective state than it has been.

Thank you for reading. Those of you who know my work also know of my dry, tongue-in-cheek humor, which plays a role here, but please understand these are true accounts of events as I experienced them.
Suzanne A. Ries R. N., M.S. N.

Acknowledgments

I wish to acknowledge all of my nursing instructors and I
 dedicate this book to them. I especially wish to thank Mrs.
Bertha Reynolds for her patience and hard work at Boston
City Hospital School of Nursing . I remember her often
saying: " I'm not going to let any student get my blood
pressure up!" Thank you to all of my nurse mentors and friends
who helped me learn.

<u>Dedication</u>

I dedicate this book to my nursing students at Pasco Hernando State College . May you thrive in your profession and be a positive role model for others.

Can I Retire Now?   A Nurse's True Story

STOP NURSE BURNOUT

CHAPTER ONE

Redefining Retirement

The current growth of the sixty-five and older population in the U.S., driven by the baby boomer generation, is unprecedented in history. The number of Americans sixty-five and older is projected to double from fifty-two million in 2018 to ninety-five million by 2060. ("Growing Bolder," by Marc Middleton.)

The aging of the boomer generation could fuel more than a fifty percent increase in seniors requiring nursing home care from one million in 2017 to about two million in 2030.

A recent survey found thirty-four percent of nurses say they will likely leave their roles by the end of 2022, with forty-four percent citing burnout and a high-stress environment as reasons for their desire to leave. The Covid19 pandemic took a major toll on nurses, causing many, especially hospital workers, to quit their jobs.

Low projected rates of new nurses, with increased patient demand related to Covid19 and an aging population, are expected to increase the nursing shortage by 2025. Without action, by 2025, two hundred thousand to four hundred and fifty thousand nurses are expected to leave the profession.

This book is written by a nurse about the problems we run into in the field of nursing. After reading it, you will have a good idea of why people enter the nursing profession and why they leave it. This is my way of taking action on burnout among nurses because the public needs to be informed of this problem so something can be done.

What if I'm too old to hire?
Does this mean I must retire?
Give up dreams which I desire?
While dressed in funereal attire?
Dreading the date I might expire?

What happens if I do not want to be: a retiree??

"Retirement" is defined as withdrawal, the removal of something from service or use. Our culture believes we reach a point of diminished skills, stamina, and ability at a certain age. Congrats! Let's give you a gold watch for achieving your long-desired retirement from our company. Now, you can busy yourself playing bingo and doing crossword puzzles.

But, we baby boomers, born between the end of WWII and the mid-1960s, rebelled against the traditional retirement age of sixty-five. We are crushing outdated social norms and redefining a life stage offering new options to benefit future generations.

In 1935, the U.S. passed the Social Security Act that specified sixty-five as the age at which retirees could expect to receive full benefits. The life expectancy in 1935 was only sixty-two, so the average American died three years before they became eligible for these benefits!

Is it any wonder, for generations, many people assumed reaching retirement age resulted in a quick transition from relaxing to withdrawal, then to declining? Retirement became like hospice, a chance to make yourself comfortable at home while getting your affairs in order, awaiting a rapidly approaching death.

In the 1960s, the average age of a nursing home resident was sixty-five, while, in 2019, it was eighty-one. It is understandable why we've developed a psychologically detrimental connection between the age of sixty-five, the idea of retirement, and the negative mindset associated with decline.

Retirement should not be considered the beginning of the end but the beginning of what's next. You are the one who should choose what's next. We boomers are in the process of creating a new belief system that will redefine retirement. We must overcome fear with action. We must view retirement as a "pit stop", the time to stop for a moment to prepare for the next stage of our race. It is a time to refuel, change tires and strategize. Every pit stop must end the same way, by stepping on the gas and pulling back onto the racetrack—not by shutting down the engine and giving up.

Retirement simply means your job no longer defines who you are, just as being an "empty-nester" means your children no longer define you; or If you are divorced or widowed, your spouse no longer defines you.

While finances are important in retirement, meaning must come before money. Most of us will need to find a way to get paid. But we need to get paid for doing things that make us want to spring out of bed every morning. Even those who have enough money to live comfortably to age one hundred without working should pursue personal growth. When we stop growing, we become old.

Comedian George Burns booked a date to play both the Caesars Palace in Las Vegas and the Palladium in London for his one-hundredth birthday.
"How can I die? I'm booked!" became one of his famous lines. The week he turned one hundred, Burns had to cancel both shows because he didn't feel well. He died a few months later. Those who knew him best said continuing to book dates is what kept him active, engaged, and enjoying life up to the century milestone he achieved.

Research into rates of mortality shows the later we retire, the longer we live. Without purpose and self-discipline, we are more prone to develop unhealthy habits such as drinking, over-eating, becoming physically inactive, and not socializing.

Many employers are actively pushing older workers out the door. Few are willing to hire senior employees because they've been branded by the ageist propaganda machine as undesirable, with diminishing skills and increasing needs. We boomers need to stand against ageism and demand equal employment opportunities.

Reading the passages above from Marc Middleton's book, "Growing Bolder" I became encouraged. I realized, as a member of the boomer generation, I did not stand alone. Many others also despised the culture of ageism in which we live.

I have always been offended by tacky "over-the-hill" ageist birthday cards, as well as jokes about seniors. I view joining AARP as the equivalent of giving up. Ask anyone what it means to be a member of AARP, and they will answer: " I'm getting old."

I also realized my dream to start a new career and retire from my nursing job fit into the philosophy outlined in this book. Middleton emphasizes the importance of finding a way to earn an income while working at your dream job.

So, I spent some time looking back on my life to discover my true passion and remembered volunteering to teach English to Italian immigrants in Boston's North End. As a student in the teaching program at Tufts University, I spent my time completing student teaching requirements at local Boston schools. This volunteer job took place in the evening, once a week for a few hours.

My love for teaching languages grew and I often conversed with my students in Italian, after taking a class in Italian at Tufts where I learned to speak well enough to make myself understood. My passion for teaching English prevailed despite the fact I didn't get paid to do it.

I studied French in elementary school and loved speaking it. Often begging my mother to take me to French restaurants to experience the food, I became a definite "Francophile." My dream came true when I went to France in the summer of

1968 with a college friend and rented a Renault. We drove to seven countries, making my first trip to Europe an exciting adventure, fueled by my ability to speak French fluently.

I studied Latin in elementary school, which planted the seeds of my love for romance languages and helped me develop an ear for them. At Wheaton College, I ended up majoring in Classics. I changed from an English major in my junior year and studied ancient Greek at Harvard summer school, despite my parents' protests. By achieving a solid "A" in this course, I proved to myself I could do it. The aptitude tests showed I scored high in the ability to learn a foreign language at the same rate as I learned English.

Having gone on to also learn Italian and Spanish, in the late 1980s, I signed up to join a hiking/photography trip to Costa Rica where I met a man who taught me elementary Spanish. I found the romance languages of French, Italian, and Spanish easy to learn and spoke well enough to understand and to be understood. Learning languages became my passion and I spoke them whenever I could.

After graduating from nursing school in 1980, I spent forty-four years working as a nurse. For the majority of those years, I specialized in psychiatric nursing and even attained a master's degree in psychiatric nursing from Yale University in 1985.

Nursing had never been my dream, but my mother's dream for me. When my favorite uncle Junie died in the early 1970s, leaving me the money for nursing school, I enlisted in nursing boot camp in 1973 and never looked back. First, I graduated from Boston City Hospital School of Nursing as a licensed practical nurse in 1974 and worked in hospitals in Massachusetts and Florida. Going on to become a registered nurse, graduating from Newton Wellesley Hospital School of Nursing in 1980.

The classroom academics came easily to me, but I despised the clinical part. The instructors often acted mean and tough and resented those of us who already had college degrees. I felt like the proverbial "square peg trying to fit myself into a round hole". Most of the time, I downright hated it. They don't call it "nurses training" for nothing.

But, I refused to quit and eventually passed with flying colors.

I wanted my mother's approval. Somewhere, in the back of my mind, Uncle Junie would pop up, encouraging me all the way.

Fast forward to 2019 when I went on a cruise to Cozumel and met a Cuban lady who suggested I apply for ESL jobs because lots of companies in China looked for people like me with master's degrees. Rich Chinese paid big bucks to American English teachers to teach their children English. All of this happened before the Covid19 pandemic.

As a result, in 2020, during the height of Covid19, at the age of seventy-five, I enrolled in a Zoom class taught by Oxford Seminars to obtain a one-hundred-twenty-hour teaching certificate allowing me to teach English as a second language. Before this, I taught several students on my own at the library. I hoped this ESL certification would lead to my teaching many students and eventually allow me to retire from nursing.

But Covid19 changed everything. Jobs in China shut down as a result. From 2020 to 2022, I searched in vain for ESL agency jobs online. Competition became fierce because many American teachers left their jobs behind to work from home. Suddenly, everyone looked for ESL teaching jobs online. I became very discouraged. But I refused to quit on my dream. I wanted to work at MY dream job and stop living someone else's dream for me.

I placed a free ad in Tampa Bay Lifestyles and received a phone call from an ISE administrator Sandra Testo. This referral landed me five online ESL students, each from a different country. I loved teaching these teenagers via Zoom. I hired a Zoom expert and quickly learned the new technology.

I loved teaching ESL to these students because each student came from a different country and culture and I could converse with them in French or Spanish.
Raquel, from Spain, remained my student the longest. Her father paid for her twice a week online English lessons for six months. I became so excited when Raquel understood my Spanish because speaking her native language helped us bond more quickly. She ended up giving me a great reference which I later used on my ESL website.

In 2021, I worked in both nursing and teaching because I didn't yet have enough students to retire from nursing. In 2022, I still had no immediate plans to leave nursing.

But, the universe had other plans for me. A right knee replacement surgery in May of 2021 forced me to take a three-month hiatus from my nursing job. Then, in April of the following year, I fell at home and ended up needing more surgery. Physical therapy helped me get back on my feet. I worked out daily on the stationary bike, walked, and did my exercises rigorously. But all this resulted in another three-month leave of absence from nursing.

I started back to work on August 8, but when September 1st came around, I still had not seen one single patient. My paychecks dwindled to almost nothing. Discouraging indeed.

I knew in my heart I didn't want to return to work in home health. A car accident in 2018 left me with a broken wrist and necessitated the purchase of a new car to replace my severely damaged vehicle. The driver who hit me ran a red light. When it happened, I'd donned my scrubs and left to see a patient.

As a result of the accident, driving around to see patients registered alarm bells in my head because I never knew what crazy driver would turn up next to do me harm. So I began to limit the distance I drove to see patients, but truly my heart ached to stop doing it altogether.

Now, four years later, my heart still isn't in it. I dread the thought of returning to my job because this means I have to drive around to see patients again.

A wise Reiki Master friend told me to listen to my heart. She told me to leave the nursing job to follow my passion to teach English and the money would follow. She advised me to write a love letter to my dream job to manifest my dream.

The next evening, around 6 PM, I sat down on our couch to write a love letter to my dream job. I became so absorbed in this task, I ignored the intense knocking at the door. When the person spoke, I thought I recognized the voice of the salesman pedaling solar energy who had pestered us last week.

"Go away, we're not interested," I hollered through the closed door.

The next thing I knew, several texts appeared magically on my phone. They said they had been knocking at the door because I did not answer my phone and they came to learn English.

I texted them back and we made a date for Saturday. They turned out to be from Puerto Rico. We met for one hour and the potential student purchased a Ventures book at his level on eBay after taking a placement test to determine the degree of English he already knew. They agreed to return when his book arrived for more classes.

After this, I became convinced the universe had finally gotten on my side and had begun to send English students my way. Also, Sandra Testo answered my email, saying she would send me online ESL students because they had already begun arriving. The next day, the host mother of a Russian boy called me to schedule ESL classes for him. The tide, at last, turned in my favor.

CHAPTER TWO

CRAZY CO-WORKERS

Nurses cite a stressful work environment as a key reason for leaving the profession. One factor creating stress is dealing with challenging coworkers. Since I entered into the nursing profession in 1974 as an L.P.N., (which stands for "low-paid nurse,") I have known my share of coworkers who contributed in a major way to my stress level. These negative experiences are listed here in chronological order:

1. In the early 1970s, while still a naive, idealistic new nurse, I worked at a state hospital in Massachusetts on the evening shift of a geriatric ward. My supervisor placed me in charge of an all-black staff, mostly Haitians.

I asked one of the aides, "Can you help me change a patient?" To my alarm and confusion, she suddenly pulled out a knife and aimed it straight at me. I glanced around for a hiding place. I had the medication room keys with me so I ran straight into the med station to get away from her and locked the door behind me, my heart pounding in my ears.

When the night shift staff arrived, I went to do the narcotic count with the charge nurse and told her what happened.

"You need to notify the supervisor immediately. These Haitian girls can be scary," she said. We made the call from the medication room together. In the end, the supervisor reprimanded this worker and suspended her for just one week from work without pay.

The other Haitians all rallied to her cause, clustering together babbling to one another in their native French. They glared at me with open hostility because I caused one of their own to get suspended. I thought she should have been fired, and perhaps today she would have been, but back then, people were more lenient on immigrants. I think of this incident from time to time when I hear about various killings and wonder if she ever went on to do anyone any real harm.

I left that job soon afterward because I didn't feel safe. I felt the Administration let me down, giving me such an impossible assignment to start with. I blamed the supervisor for placing me in charge of that ward. From that point on, I learned to put my safety first. Never again did I accept such a difficult job from an Administrator who appeared unconcerned about my welfare.

2. My next bad memory of crazy coworkers occurred at Veterans' Administration hospitals in the mid-1980s. I graduated from Yale School of Nursing with a M.S.N. Degree in psychiatric nursing. I wanted to help veterans, so I applied and got accepted at a V.A. hospital in Massachusetts near Lexington, where I lived at the time in my childhood home with my parents.

In the 1980s, V.A. hospitals had difficult working conditions. They have improved since then, but back then, on the unit where I worked, patients could still smoke on the wards.

This presented a huge problem for me because I had allergies to cigarette smoke.

Most of the V.A. nurses intended to stay in the system for a long time to collect a government pension when they retired. Unlike me, most of them did not have graduate degrees but received promotions for their years of service, including my direct supervisor.

She and I locked horns from the day we met. We worked on an all-male, mostly geriatric unit. "Nurse Ratchet," as we called her behind her back, enjoyed zipping up flies on the pants of her passive subjects. She loved to give orders and treated her "ancillary staff" (her words) with disrespect and abhorrence.

The cigarette smoke billowing through the air caused me to choke so badly I didn't even last a year at that place. I transferred to the Boston V.A. Hospital three months after I started. They had an opening on the night shift for a Charge Nurse of the substance abuse unit. Since this job paid well, I accepted it even though I found it difficult to adjust to working the eleven to seven shift.

At this hospital, they required patients to smoke in the lobby rather than on the floors. In the lobby, on a normal day, one could see at least fifty or more men all dressed in pajamas smoking, like pre-war chimneys.

In my interview with the charge nurse, I said, "I don't want to take this position unless you provide me with a male coworker. I don't feel safe alone on this unit at night with all-male substance abusers as patients."

"Of course, of course. I completely understand. Don't worry, we will make sure you are not working alone," she assured me.

However, when I showed up the first night for the job, I found no coworker, male or otherwise. I spent the night alone. All night long, I heard the men's room door opening and closing many times and felt sure they must be doing drug deals in there but didn't dare to check.

My next conversation with the charge R.N. did not go well.

I asked, "Why did no coworker show up to work with me?"

She said," Because the administration was not willing to provide the "extra staff." I quit that job then and there because she lied and I still felt unsafe.

3. My last and final job with crazy coworkers in Massachusetts happened on a psychiatric unit at Malden Hospital in Malden, Massachusetts on the evening shift. I worked as the medications nurse and my coworker filled the supervisor role.

We heard in the change of shift report about one of the patients being very drug-seeking, demanding extra Valium in addition to her regular doses. Her treatment team wanted her to cut back on this narcotic for health reasons. The Valium-seeking patient asked me for extra medication.

I explained, "Your team wants you to cut back on the Valium for your own good, so you can become less dependent on it."

But this patient didn't buy it. In anger, she wrapped several towels around her neck to choke herself in protest for not getting the extra pills.

"I'll do it, I'll choke myself if you don't give me the extra pills," she threatened in anger and pulled on the towels around her neck.

My coworker became alarmed and said, "We need to fill out an incident report because she attempted a suicidal gesture."

"I know this patient had no real intent to choke herself to death with towels. She's just testing us and trying to get her way. We don't need to fill out an incident report. She is faking."

"I don't care what you say. We need to fill out a report for our own sake to cover our own butts." she insisted.

We unwrapped the towels but the patient remained hostile and volatile. At the end of the shift, I cosigned the incident report but did not have a chance to read through the whole thing because I had to be at work at seven the next morning.

Early the next morning, I received a call from my supervisor.

"Don't bother coming into work, Suzanne. We are suspending you for three days. The medical director and I will meet with you in my office tomorrow at nine am."

By the time I met with them, I shook like a leaf and my stomach kept doing flip-flops. I needed this job for the money.

How would I pay my bills if they suspended me for three days without pay?

They said, "Your coworker wrote in the report you caused the patient to make a suicidal gesture by withholding her Valium from her."

I explained "That is not what happened. It's not true. The patient received her regular prescribed doses of Valium but demanded extra pills from me as well. This represented extra narcotics her treatment team didn't want her to have. Why would you believe my coworker before even hearing my side of the story?" They had nothing to say.

Suddenly, a voice from somewhere inside me squeaked, "I QUIT."

"But we don't want you to quit. We just want to teach you a lesson," the supervisor said.

" I QUIT." This time, my voice grew louder and I became more enraged with their unjust treatment. I resigned that day and left their office.

The next day I received a phone call from the hospital Administrator saying, "I want to see you in my office as soon as possible."

When I met with him, he said, "We are having problems in that psychiatric unit. What can I do to help you?"

Since I already knew I wanted to move to Florida, I said, "I want unemployment compensation." and he agreed. This enabled my dream of moving to Florida to come true. For two years, I received $1200 a month from the state of Massachusetts. The coworker who thought she had stabbed me in the back ended up handing me my dream on a silver platter.

Later, after I met with the administrator, I celebrated with my friend, Barbara .who had also worked on that unit.

We went to her house and her wise mother told us: "Every kick is a boost!" For the next month, Barb and I met weekly for lunch to laugh and celebrate our departure from that awful unit.

Every time I encounter adversity, I still remember how God moved in such a mysterious way to enable me to move to Florida and I remember to say, " Every kick is a boost!"

So, the next time a crazy friend or coworker kicks you, remember what happened to me. That kick could turn out to be a boost in disguise. Don't let it get you down. Remember to say, "Every kick is a boost!"

4. Moving to Florida in 1992, I took a job working as an R.N. for a home health company in Sarasota. They assigned me to a psychiatric patient living on Siesta Key beach, who battled skin cancer.

About two weeks after I started seeing her, this patient complained about leg pain shooting down from her spine. I told my supervisor and documented this in my notes, but no one had time to listen. They were too busy dealing with other matters.

A month later, I received a phone call from the big boss saying, "Come into my office immediately. You are in a lot of trouble."

As it turned out, this patient had a massive tumor in her spine pressing on her nerves causing her to have pain. They wanted me to rewrite all my clinical notes to indicate they addressed this physical problem and did something about it.

"Isn't that illegal?" I asked the supervisors innocently. No one answered my question but insisted I rewrite all of my motes or I would be fired on the spot.

Then, they said, "A neighbor complained to the state that you left the patient over the weekend covered in urine and feces."

"Not true, I last saw her on Friday and I left her clean at the time after showering her and putting her into clean clothes. " I told them.

A state inspector called me to say he wanted to meet with me. I feared I could lose my nursing license if found guilty of negligence with this patient. This scared me to death because I did attempt to communicate with my supervisors many times about this patient's condition, but no one listened to me. Now, they treated me like a criminal, but I knew I had done nothing wrong.

The state inspector said, "The family decided not to pursue the case any further, so the state no longer needs to be involved. I think you acted prudently and had committed no harm at all to the patient."

I ended up leaving that job shortly afterward, disgusted and disillusioned. They forced me to rewrite my clinical notes, which I knew to be illegal. This experience left a bad taste in my mouth because my supervisor and coworkers browbeat me into doing something I did not want to do. Making the agency look good on paper had become their only concern, and saving their skins at the expense of mine.

5. My next coworker's nightmare occurred at a psychiatric hospital in Manatee County, Florida. I accepted a position as the only R.N. in an outpatient substance abuse unit. When I started, my predecessor had already left, so I had no one to orient me to the job. I set up the file cabinet on my own, organizing all the paperwork into folders.

The most positive aspect of this position turned out to be my role as a teacher. My duties included teaching classes to the patients as well as testing urine daily for drugs. I worked closely with the psychiatrists who prescribed their medications.

My direct supervisor described himself as a "recovering alcoholic." His supervisor described herself as an "ex-Heroin addict." They both belonged to Alcoholics Anonymous and Narcotics Anonymous.

When they interviewed me, they asked, "Have you ever abused drugs or alcohol?" I answered, "No, I drink wine occasionally" and they both scowled at me, indicating their displeasure.

"We're not sure you are appropriate for the position. All of our staff are members of either A.A. or N.A. and most are former addicts because they empathize better with our clients."

In the entire building of over fifty people, I, and a counselor named Ron were the only ones, not former substance abusers. It seemed being an addict or a former addict earned you a badge of honor here.

When the big boss interviewed me, she told me frankly about the Hepatitis-C she had contracted because of shooting up with dirty needles. She injected herself daily with an antiviral medication called Interferon to survive. I did wonder why her skin looked so yellow and why she looked emaciated.

My immediate supervisor confided in me he desired to drink again. Two months after I started the job, he fell off the wagon and went back to drinking. He showed up six months later after graduating from rehab.

I drove an old difficult-to-start car. When I arrived late for work as a result, my supervisor cruelly ridiculed me and my car.

"Get a horse !" he screamed at me with contempt. I managed to stay at this job for two years despite some major run-ins with my two dysfunctional supervisors and a female psychiatrist who tried to get me fired because she thought I didn't treat her with proper respect. When I learned she wrote prescriptions for painkillers and other narcotics for the staff, I lost all respect for her. Back in Massachusetts, this would be illegal. I had already learned, in Florida, things operated differently, and illegal activities were frequently tolerated because no one checked up to stop them from happening. In my book, they call that backward. I quickly learned the state of Florida had a backward mental health care system.

In Massachusetts, the mental health system provides excellent care to the rich and poor alike. It is supported by hefty state taxes, but, in Florida, they have no state taxes to compensate for mental health services.

The big boss said, "I plan to cut your lunch hour from one hour to half an hour soon. And you will be required to work the evening shift instead of the day shift because we are starting a new evening program." All of this made me very unhappy because I felt my supervisors intentionally tried to make my life more difficult. They behaved mean-spirited and unkind to me.

" Oh God, please help me find a way out of this job because the stress is becoming unbearable." I prayed daily. Breakthrough came when I turned sixty and inherited some family money.

I went to Primm Valley, Utah with my Amway team and took a picture of a sign reading: "SUZANNE WON $250,000!" I posted this photo on my office door the day I left that horrible job with the dysfunctional psychiatrist and supervisors. Patients came up to congratulate me for winning all the money. It was payback time because I drove away in a brand-new purple PT Cruiser!

CHAPTER THREE

NURSE DESPOTS

" We have met the enemy and he is us"(Pogo)

On the website LinkedIn, the Nurses' Nook Group posts comments from nurses. Today on this site, Sara Fung, R.N. posted: " Please brag about a thing you did in 2022 that you're proud of. "

Elizabeth Wunderllick, PACU R.N. posted this as her accomplishment:

"Wrote Governor Ron Desantis about bullying in the nursing profession. I have worked in a wide variety of clinical areas and this issue is widespread and needs to be exposed for what it is ... unprofessional. I wrote that this issue needs to move from the private sector to the public eye so that legislation can come against it."

At least twenty-five to fifty others, including myself, responded with their reactions to being bullied, citing it as the main reason they disliked their jobs so much.

These current comments on LinkedIn show bullying as an ever-present dragon lurking in every school of nursing, hospital, and other areas such as agencies and doctors' offices where nurses work. This problem will not go away soon because of systemic issues. Nurse bullies are not born that way because bullying is a learned behavior. We become bullies because we are bullied by others.

The very first introduction to the profession occurs in schools of nursing where young women and men become indoctrinated into the ways of the culture. Many teachers bully their students because that is what they experienced at the hands of their instructors.

I know several instructor bullies and suffered my share of them. As a student at Massachusetts General Hospital School of Nursing in the early 1970s, several of these female tyrants persecuted a group of us, all college graduates who entered the profession after achieving degrees in other fields. I believe these teachers, jealous of our education levels, became determined to show their superior smarts by executing games of unprofessional one-upmanship. The worst of the lot, Ms. Kenney, flunked me by one point in my clinical rotation to show her superior intellectual prowess. In retrospect, I should have sued the school and demanded they return my tuition money.

I will never forget this prim and proper instructor, with her starched white cap perched high on her head. She reminded me of an ostrich. My stomach flip-flopped when she came around because she intimidated me so badly. She often snuck up behind us to spy on our communication with patients.

"You seem unsure of yourself," she said to me, her pale slashes of eyebrows knitted together to make her look extra cross.

"If you need to review a procedure, there is a manual at the nurses' station, " she growled and slapped the chart she carried against her thigh for emphasis. She never understood my terror of her menacing bully behavior.

I vowed to retaliate. When I accepted the position of Adjunct Instructor at Pasco State College in the School of Nursing, I knew my chance had arrived. I determined to become a positive role model for the students as a type of healing for the wounds I endured at the hands of nurse tyrants. I received positive feedback from my students and remained friends with them even after I stepped down from that position. One former student attended my wedding years later in the smoky mountains of Tennessee.

In the previous chapter, I described the bully V.A. nurse who supervised me at the Bedford V.A. Hospital in Bedford, Massachusetts. I also told you about the despots at the Sarasota agency who coerced me into rewriting my paperwork to save their skins. I should have hired a lawyer to defend my rights and refused to commit this illegal act. But you know what they say about hindsight, it is always 20/20.

I met another oppressor at the Visiting Nurses Association in the early 1990s when I lived in Hernando County Florida. My former supervisor had been fantastic, orienting me to the complicated online Medicare Oasis forms of home health. When Kathy left, we received a warning her successor would not be nearly as nice.

This turned out to be a gross understatement. Kathy's replacement appeared determined to persecute me no matter how hard I tried to please her. She presided over staff conferences like a dictator, determined to undermine nurses and glorify the accomplishments of the physical therapists.

Trained as a psychiatric nurse, my problem became one of getting enough patients. Once again, to earn enough income, I found myself forced to work with medical patients who often required technical procedures I had not done in a long while. I also had to work weekends and this meant taking on new admissions. Frequently, on a Sunday, I became swamped with three starts of care. Considering each admission took a minimum of two hours, three meant six hours of work. Sometimes, I called the patients to ask if they would prefer a Monday visit and they often consented. The new nurse manager did not like my doing this because it meant the marketer who referred that patient would not receive her weekend bonus.

My tormentor took her final opportunity to screw me royally when she assigned me to an A.L.F. out in the middle of nowhere. There, supposed "chronically ill psychiatric patients" live under supervision. This A.L.F. turned out to be a full hundred miles from my house and the drive took me over tortuous hills and bumpy dirt back roads.

When I arrived, the place looked dark and foreboding. The building appeared to be old and falling. Holding back my horror at the dilapidation of the place, I parked my car and walked into the building.

"Hello," I said to the hostile-looking nurse who greeted me. I pasted a smile on my face and did my best to appear friendly. Unmoved, she stared back at me and said, "Yes? How can I help you?"

"I am here to see a new patient for the start of care, of Mr. A. Smith"

"He is not here. He is at a medical appointment."

"But I called last night to make sure he would be here since the distance out here is so great. The staff member I spoke with assured me he would be available."

"Who did you speak to?" she asked in a surly tone.

"I've no idea of her name, I didn't write it down. But surely she would have checked his chart to see his schedule before telling me this," I retorted in equal agitation.

"I can't help you if you don't know who you spoke to."
"Well, It appears the level of professionalism here is just as dilapidated as the building itself. This is disgraceful," I responded with equal hostility, lashing out at the employee and this filthy place I had somehow ended up in through no fault of my own.

Needless to say, this ugly interaction caused an unhappy chain of events. The employee complained to my nurse despot manager and I received termination papers soon after that. Thus ended my illustrious career with the Visiting Nurses

Association. After this, I made a promise to myself to waste no more of my time working under the management of tyrants.

As long as I can remember, people often quote this saying among nurses "Nurses eat their young alive." Judith Meissner, RN, MSN coined this phrase in a 1986 article she wrote to describe the hostility young nurses face at the hands of their more experienced coworkers. A survey taken in October 2021 found that 93% of all healthcare employees have either experienced or witnessed bullying behavior Statistics say 60% of new nurses quit their first jobs before the end of the first year because of the bad behavior of coworkers.

Published on October 13, 2021, Renee Thompson wrote an article entitled "Why Do Nurses Bully Each Other?" Bullying is pervasive and destructive in every industry. However, nurses are supposed to treat their patients with kindness. Why then are we so mean to one another? Thompson has become a bullying expert and has written many articles regarding this subject.

Published in the "Nursing Administration Quarterly" July/September issue, Cole Edmonson's article entitled " Our Own Worst Enemies, The Nurse Bullying Epidemic," cites how negative nurse behavior exacerbates the nursing shortage, contributes to a poor nurse work environment, increases the risk to patients, lowers patient satisfaction scores and creates greater nurse turnover which costs the average hospital $4 million to $7 million per year. She advocates raising awareness about the problem of bullying, mitigating contributing factors, and enforcing a strong anti-bullying policy. She recommends nurses actively work to change the culture because bullying has no place in the nursing profession or healthcare. She states this nurse bullying issue is well-documented in clinical and leadership literature. Bullying starts early, pervading the classroom from bedside to boardroom.

One study taken over six months showed 78% of students experienced bullying in nursing school. Nurse bullying occurs in almost all care settings from the patient floor to the executive suite. In one 2018 study, 60% of all managers, directors, and executives said they experienced bullying at the job site and 26% called the bullying "severe."

Also known as "horizontal hostility," "relational aggression," and "lateral violence," the American Nurses Association defines nurse bullying as: "repeated, unwanted harmful actions intended to humiliate, offend, and cause distress in the recipient, calling it "a very serious issue that threatens patient safety, RN safety, and the nursing profession as a whole." (Edmonson, "Our Worst Enemies: The Nurse Bullying Epidemic.")

Edmonson divides these negative behaviors into two categories: covert and overt. Overt bullying is easier to recognize, including micromanaging, verbal criticism, name-calling, insults, and direct threats. Covert bullying is passive-aggressive and can include rumors, gossip, unfair assignments, low grades, or undesirable tasks as punishment and sabotage.

I experienced more covert bullying than overt. When working at Pasco State Community College, I was forced to leave this job due to the unkind behavior of my fellow nursing instructors who ridiculed me for my teaching techniques not being "up to date." They could have just as easily shown me more kindness by demonstrating some of the techniques they used, but instead, they chose to bully me until I felt forced into leaving the job.

I can list other examples of bullying by uncaring, unprofessional, co-workers. When I worked at the Cares Agency, I told the manager about my role as a psychiatric R.N. and my subsequent lack of experience in wound care. Why then did she assign me to a little Hitler who expected me to mimic her perfectly packed dressing wound care technique on my first attempt? She then assigned me to another nasty one for the same dressing change. Then, both of them put me down and ridiculed my attempt to follow their examples of wound care techniques. Feeling ganged up on, I quit that job in no time.

The D.O.N. confronted me the next day after my feeble try at the packed wound dressing fizzled out. Her round face scowled at me and she rose in her seat shouting at me like a ferocious mother grizzly bear defending her territory.

"I've heard from my staff that you are unable to perform wound care. You are fired!"

I looked her straight in the eye and said, " I told you when we first met that wound care is not my specialty because I have been doing psych nursing for so long. Obviously, you did not listen."

Another time, Encourage sent me into an assisted living facility to administer an injection to a patient. The routine ALF nurse always met me with a hostile negative attitude, especially if I happened to arrive during her lunch hour, forcing her to retrieve the shot from the medicine cart on her time off. She often blew up at me, muttering hostile remarks under her breath. I dreaded going there as a result.

"It's you again, always showing up at the wrong time. " Her fat pig-like face glowered at me all the while. She reminded me of a wild boar in heat.

I jumped for joy when I heard that the patient died.

Interestingly, micromanaging is listed as a type of overt bullying behavior. The employees of my last supervisor often accused her of micromanaging their patients. Several of my coworkers left the company for other jobs., citing her and her micromanaging as their reason for leaving.

If we want to solve the nursing shortage, many negative issues must be addressed but the first problem to tackle must be nurse bullying. If we, as nurses, cannot treat one another with respect, then how can we expect to receive the praise we deserve from others? How can we expect to prove we are deserving of better wages and working conditions when we downgrade one another? Like Pogo says in the cartoon: "We have met the enemy and he is us."

CHAPTER FOUR

Dysfunctional Hospitals

I previously stated how backward the mental health system is in Florida compared to Massachusetts due to a lack of funding from state taxes. In this chapter, I describe two such hospitals and my experiences working there.

Following the mistake of buying a home in Brooksville, Florida in 2005, I worked at a facility in Hernando County accepting Baker-Acted patients from within a fifty-mile radius. Springbrook Hospital exemplified archaic working conditions at this time. At this hospital, three wards existed: one served as a kind of "intensive care unit" for the most acute patients, the second consisted of mostly chronic mentally-ill geriatric clients, while a third, the Admissions Unit, functioned as a holding place for patients when they first arrived before being assigned to one of the other two wards.

The strong stench of urine and fresh feces greeted me when I first arrived at the geriatric unit, by far the worst of the three units. This smell permeated the walls, the floors, the furniture, and everything else within sight. Here, staff restrained elderly patients in strait jackets, and nurses medicated them with anti-psychotic medicines like Thorazine. This caused them to fall asleep in chairs with trays attached to the front, drooling onto their hospital gowns. They spent all day long in these chairs and sometimes during the night. They ate, drank, urinated, and defecated in these chairs because the staff did not take the time to walk them to the bathroom or check their diapers to see if they needed changing.

On the acute unit, many screaming clients greeted me. When they originally arrived, they needed their medications and often did not get them. Frequently, a loud buzzer sounded to alert all staff to come to help out in a crisis. Then, strong male workers held the patient down in a secluded room until the nurse arrived with a tranquilizer injection to calm them down.

My only positive experience at this hospital occurred in the Admissions Unit. There I could escape from the urine and feces odors and high-pitched screams. Hence, I managed to think more clearly. I liked my supervisor. She protected her staff from the bullies at the top and treated us with respect and compassion.

When a coworker and I tried to start activities for the patients on the evening shift, Administration told us not to bother because funds did not exist for Bingo games. So, we supplied the money out of our pockets for the prizes to fuel their passion for Bingo. This was the first time I ever saw any patients on the geriatric unit smile. They looked forward to winning at Bingo and this gave them something to live for.

I ended up leaving Springbrook when I transitioned into home health care. I made this decision because a coworker told me about Senior Home Care posting an ad for psychiatric nurses.

When she recruited me for this job, I went with her to interview for a position.

Before this, I had one other brief negative experience at a place in Pasco County called The Harbour, providing treatment to adults, young adults, and seniors 65 or older. I recall the unusual layout. The staff sat or stood behind a gigantic desk called the "nurses' station," with the medication room located in the back. Patients stood or sat on chairs in a glass-enclosed room across from the nurses' station.

The only interaction staff had with patients occurred during medication times. When I first started at this hospital, I made the mistake of stepping into the patient's glass bubble and talking to one of them.

The nurse in charge admonished me, saying, "We don't talk to them. We just medicate them."

I thought about the advanced psychiatric units in Massachusetts where I had worked. Most of them had "milieu therapy" where patients and staff interacted together in therapeutic ways. What a stark contrast to this backward approach of "us versus them" at the Harbour Hospital.

51

CHAPTER FIVE

Challenging Patients

"Borderline" is not just a song by Madonna. The Mayo Clinic online site defines "Borderline Personality Disorder" as " a mental health disorder impacting the way you feel about yourself and others, causing problems functioning in everyday life. It includes self-image issues, difficulty managing emotions and behavior, and a pattern of unstable relationships. Symptoms include: intense fear of abandonment, inappropriate anger, and frequent mood swings that push others away, even though the desired goal is to have loving, lasting relationships. " More dangerous symptoms frequently include paranoia, impulsive behaviors such as gambling, unsafe sex, spending sprees, binge eating or drug abuse, suicidal threats, or self-injury, especially in response to fear of separation or rejection. These suicidal threats and/or gestures cause people with this disorder to enter psychiatric hospitals, frequently against their will.

While living in Massachusetts, I saw many patients with "Borderline Personality Disorder" on inpatient psychiatric units where I worked. Psychiatrists often ordered round-the-clock supervision due to their self-harming gestures. They also told the staff to draw up contracts for these patients to sign as a way to trick them into promising good behavior. I never saw these contracts work to achieve their intended goal because the clients usually ended up outsmarting the staff. They refused to be tricked into good behavior and seemingly spent every waking moment thinking up ways to torment staff. Often, workers ended up being split on how to deal with the negative behavior and so this staff-splitting became another characteristic of "Borderline Personality Disorder."

The patient I previously described who tried to choke herself by wrapping towels around her neck had a diagnosis of "Borderline Personality Disorder." If you recall, my coworker and I disagreed about whether or not she should receive the extra doses of Valium she demanded. This disagreement is called staff-splitting and it ended up causing much confusion on that psychiatric unit.

In graduate school, I wrote my thesis about clients with this problem, questioning whether or not most of them are serious in their suicidal attempts or whether these gestures are attention seeking. My advisor voiced her opinion that most patients attempt suicide as a call for help rather than as a serious effort to kill themselves. She also told us she did not believe people with this problem should be admitted to hospitals but are best treated in the community using long-term therapy with a professional therapist. She stated she had acted as a therapist with many of these patients and they did well, staying on their prescribed medications. She said these patients require long term therapy because the root of their problems normally go back to their childhoods. Therapy serves as a type of "re-parenting" and so a bond of trust must first be established between client and therapist.

After I worked in home health, I encountered several patients with this diagnosis. During the years 2015 to 2017, an agency hired me to see a specific client who had been admitted with a wound. When the medical nurse assigned to this client asked her about her wound, she found out it was self-inflicted. Her medical nurse ended up quitting, leaving me alone to deal with this challenging patient.

I advised my supervisor to discharge this patient as she had become a liability to the agency due to her self-destructive behavior. Patients who are actively suicidal need hospitalization because they cannot be monitored round-the-clock by home health care workers. She agreed ,but said we would need to hook the patient up first to mental health treatment in the community. Once we achieved this, I discharged the patient. Afterward, I received several phone calls from irate supervisors within the agency saying we never should have discharged the patient because she needed help. This patient had managed to split the staff in true borderline fashion. In my opinion, this confirmed her diagnosis.

Another client who lived in East Pasco county, threatened suicide when I tried to discharge her for noncompliance with her treatment plan. When I went to her house to see her, she proudly displayed cigarette burns on both of her arms. She threatened to do more if I discharged her. I made certain to find her outpatient therapy prior to her discharge, so I discharged her and never looked back.

Are you aware that our federal government dispenses free Viagra by mail to male veterans, even those in their 80's and 90's? This often presents a definite problem. My agency sent me out to admit a psychiatric patient, a former veteran in his late 80's with a diagnosis of Dementia. He lived alone in a remote part of Hudson, far away from any neighbors. He proudly showed me a loaded gun which he kept with him at all times. When he started to brag about his sexual conquests, I began to get nervous.

That was the fastest admission I ever remember doing because I completed it in less than half an hour. I felt so anxious to escape from him and his loaded gun, I forgot to have him sign a few documents. He ended up being discharged soon afterward because the speech therapist, who refused to see any patients with guns, verbalized her displeasure at being assigned to this client. I never saw him again after his admission.

I remember admitting another challenging client who had been recently discharged from the Trinity Hospital behavioral health unit. He had a diagnosis of Psychotic Depression. His wife, who worked as a nurse, verbalized her panic to me because her husband did not seem any better than when he first entered the hospital.

"He thinks I'm tape recording our conversations," she told me.

When I spoke with her husband, his paranoid imagination revealed itself.

He said, "I don't feel comfortable talking to you because the cameras and microphones all over my house are recording and videotaping our interactions and conversations."

I told his wife, "I think he's been discharged too soon from the hospital. He's still psychotic because he thinks we are recording him."

His wife had to provide supervision for him because of his delusional condition. As a result of my biweekly visits, she finally returned to her hospital job. She verbalized her gratitude to me because she said her husband was driving her nuts.

It surprised me he'd been discharged when he still showed signs of delusional thinking. In the 1980's, when I worked on psychiatric units in Massachusetts, patients were never released into the community until their psychosis had cleared and they were no longer delusional. I remembered attending case conferences where doctors discussed the patients in detail along with their treatment which often included anti-psychotic medications to clear their thinking. I remembered clearly how one psychiatrist became upset because he felt the insurance companies began telling him when to discharge his patients.

Insurance companies now dictate length of stay instead of the healthcare providers. Frequently, as in the case of this client, patients are discharged because their insurance has run out and not because they are better.

If you Google search "Are psychiatric nurses hard to find?"you will see this answer. Diana Sarabia Gallagher, a psych nurse since 1989 states: "I think there a few reasons why it's hard to find a job in psych nursing and also why it's hard to keep a job in psych nursing.

It's emotionally draining to work with patients who often can't be reasoned with. They hear things you don't hear and see things you can't see and sometimes have irrational fears phobias, rituals. You have to be on your guard every second.

It can be physically dangerous and the danger is unpredictable. One patient I remember was a teenage girl on a suicide watch. A nurse was blow drying her hair and she sat passively, not talking to anyone. Suddenly, she grabbed the cord to the blow dryer and started strangling herself with it. The nurse had no warning this would happen. The patient later said voices told her to kill herself."

My last story is of the patient who threw his psych nurse under the bus because he fell in love with another nurse. When his mental health nurse went on medical leave, he met another nurse, assigned to cover him in her absence. The original plan was for his psych nurse to see him again when she returned. But, in typical psych patient style, this man did not cooperate but instead sabotaged the plan by refusing to allow his psych nurse to see him unless the second nurse could also be present. He said he had fallen in love with his replacement nurse.

While not actively suicidal, this patient frequently reported seeing visions of his deceased wife and hearing knocking at the door when no one was there. Therefore, he definitely was someone who could not be reasoned with due to irrational fears, phobias and rituals. One had to be on their guard with him every second.

According to his mental health nurse, it all started two years prior, when her supervisor called to tell her she had a patient who badly needed mental health services. He took fifty different prescribed medications but had taken himself off many of them including Insulin and anti-psychotic meds he badly needed. He suffered from PTSD with Psychotic Depression along with multiple medical problems including COPD and Diabetes. He constantly complained of symptoms of diarrhea and dizziness. His psych nurse documented clinical notes to his doctor and his psychiatrist to keep them informed but they never changed his medications not did they advise her how to proceed with the patient.

When his psych nurse first visited him in his one bedroom apartment, cockroaches climbed out of his cluttered, filthy sink. She had great difficulty finding a clean spot to place her nurse's bag, so she ended up hanging it on his front door knob.

He looked at least ten years older than his sixty-eight years. Those years had not been kind to him.

"I'm so lonely and depressed," he told her in a pitiful manner, "I don't believe my only daughter loves me because she never has time for me."

The psych R.N. spent over two hours every visit listening to his many complaints, emotional fears and family conflicts. He told her supervisor she was the only nurse he wanted to see and he told her she was one of the few people he would allow into his house.

Meanwhile, a homemaker came to clean his place who came for thirty hours per week. The state of Florida paid for her services.

In typical psych patient style, he overstepped the boundaries of this relationship. Soon, the homemaker cooked and delivered meals for him. She confided in him her marital problems. Then, the patient told his psych nurse he had fallen in love with the homemaker and, if it were not for her jealous Cuban husband, he would run away and marry her.

When the state cut her hours back, the patient became heartbroken and told his psych nurse he didn't want to live anymore. He told her he wanted his doctor to put him back on his former antidepressant of Zoloft because the Prozac wasn't working. So, his psych nurse reported this to his doctor and psychiatrist. Just one month earlier, he had told her he wanted to be taken off the Zoloft because it contributed to his symptoms of dizziness. So, his psychiatrist had discontinued the Zoloft, prescribing Prozac instead. She documented all of this in clinical notes to doctors but it takes time for changes to occur within a medical system. Now, he had changed his mind again about his medication and she documented it all again in notes to his doctors. At this time, his psych nurse went on leave and nurse number two took over.

The last time nurse number one spoke with nurse number two,

she said the patient insisted on showing her pornography, so she couldn't wait to get rid of him.

"He's a dirty old man. I can't wait until you take him back," the replacement nurse told the psych nurse. So, it came as a complete surprise to the psych nurse when the patient refused to see her and the replacement nurse took over the case. In fact, he became downright insulting to her.

When she called him to see how he was doing, he said, "You need to retire," in a terse, perfunctory, deprecating manner.

There is a rule in the profession which states the patient always makes the rules and the patients' rights must be respected. This means you must obey the irrational rules of a psychotic psych patient, such as the one described in this true case scenario.

Is it any wonder psych nurses burn out so quickly from such emotionally draining patients? Is it any wonder why good psychiatric nurses are so hard to find?

CHAPTER SIX
Scaling the Walls to Swing From the Ivy

In 1983, when I first met my new supervisor, Cheryl, I learned she graduated from Yale School of Nursing. I pictured a serene college campus tucked away in a rural area with buildings covered in ivy. I obsessed over the pristine beauty of the place, the ivy-covered walls, and the thrill of getting a degree from an "Ivy League" institution of higher learning.

"Suzanne," Cheryl gazed at me with beautiful green eyes, their lids covered with a slash of stylish, modern, turquoise eye shadow. Flipping strands of long chestnut hair between carefully manicured nails she continued, "I had the best experience at Yale and met the most fabulous nurse mentors. I'm sure with your education and smarts, you would have no trouble getting in. I will even write you a glowing letter of reference."

Everything about Cheryl oozed beauty, self-confidence, and professional stature. The Director of Nursing of the mental health unit at Addison Gilbert Hospital, she became my role model.

I worked in Gloucester Massachusetts in the mental health department at the only hospital in the town. Gloucester, best known as the home of Gorton's seafood products, sported a huge statue of a fisherman in the town square to advertise their main industry.

Many commercial fishermen residing in Gloucester

ended up as patients in my unit, due to their problems with "chronic alcoholism."

I lived in the nearby town of Essex, best known as the home of the New England Fried Clam. These were the full-bellied clams, not the strips everyone in New England knows taste like fried rubber bands. Definitely not. These were the real thing.

Cheryl encouraged me from the beginning, saying, "Suzanne, you've worked on this unit for two years. Getting this Master's degree at Yale and studying to be a Clinical Nurse Specialist, will allow you to advance your career and get a degree from an Ivy League school."

I could think of nothing to stop me from going to Yale. My commitment-phobic boyfriend already informed me in no uncertain terms of his intentions, or lack thereof. He definitively told me exactly where he stood. He delivered his ultimatum in a cold, cruel, distant manner, absolutely void of all emotion.

63

"I am not ready to make any long-term commitment to you. If you choose to move elsewhere to pursue further education, I will have to break up with you. I don't choose to pursue a long-distance romance."

My mother, not so fondly, nicknamed him "Pisswinks" when he showed up at our house the first time. She didn't warm up to his icy, dispassionate style and never appreciated his high I.Q., his M.I.T. Computer engineering education, or his career as a highly-trained computer specialist who designed and manufactured computers. He paid cash for his house and ran his business from there. My niece, Cathy, told me he impressed her a lot because of his intelligence. He impressed me because I never met anyone before him who paid for their house with cash. It turned out my intuitive mother had the best take of all on this man.

"Pisswinks", she said, refusing to allow him to impress her. I even watched an Oprah television show about commitment-phobic men. She interviewed several and I sent for the transcript in a last-ditch attempt to understand "Pisswinks." All to no avail. I had to finally admit my mother was correct about him after all.

I could not find the word "Pisswinks" in any dictionary but got the general idea from the sound of the word. Definitely negative and suggestive of "Piss-off" which conjured up thoughts of "Commitment Phobia" to the highest degree. He was also a devout atheist, a badge he wore proudly, but a turn-off for me.

"We have nothing to prove God exists," he stated in a flat perfunctory manner. He never understood the concept of belief in God being a faith-based issue. Nor could he see the "proof" of God in small everyday things like the birth of a child, the changing of seasons, or falling in love.

So, it didn't take much for Cheryl to talk me into her Yale program. I grew tired of pissing my passion down the toilet and wasting my time on a "Pisswinks" of a man who cared more about his hardware than about his soft, sensitive female companion.

"Piss on "Pisswinks," I defiantly told myself and filled out the application in my best calligraphic style with my new silver Dr. Grip Pilot pen.

My parents said, "We completely support your decision and are on board with the idea."

"I will even pay the hefty tuition bill," Dad said. "You know we want to help you with your education and career just like we helped your two brothers." My father retired at the age of sixty-five, having achieved the CEO position at Commonwealth Energy Company, a company on the New York Stock Exchange, based in Cambridge, Massachusetts.

I knew he could well afford to pay my tuition, so I said, "Sure, Dad, that would be great. I can become your new retirement project."

Grieving the loss of his work, when my dad retired he replaced his job with a new obsession: alcohol. In 1982, I moved from Essex back to Lexington to live with my parents. I expected to find them enjoying their golden years together. Instead, they argued constantly and alcohol became the main source of conflict.

"Never did I think you would ruin your senior years and your health with Beefeater's Gin," my mother nagged when she caught him refilling his cup for the fifth time with this brew he kept hidden in the kitchen cabinet over the stove.

Dad always knew better than to answer her back. He countered by going back for a sixth refill, took his coveted cup from the kitchen into the living room, and sat in his favorite armchair, Then he turned on the TV, and sipped his gin, enjoying every drop.

I remained in denial of his problem until my brother, Bill, sounded the alarm.

He said, "I caught Dad on video at his house in Plymouth," and showed us the tape of my father slurring his words:

"I love this stuff," he said, pointing to the Gin. "I don't care what anyone thinks, because this is what I want."

Thus began my obsession to become the sleuth who uncovers the shameful secrets of my dysfunctional family. I knew my second cousin Joan had drinking issues because she confessed she spent six months at the Hazelton Rehab facility in Minnesota.

Also, I knew my Uncle Junie on my mother's side died of the drink. The police found him alone in his house in the 1970s. He died surrounded by an ugly mess of rotting food amid thousands of newspapers dating back to the 1950s. After years of telling us nothing about his problem, he spent those years hoarding newspapers and drinking himself to death. Mother tried to cover it all up, refusing to tell me the nasty, shameful truth.

We already knew her family carried the alcoholism gene, but, this latest shock of Dad's problem hit me like a ton of bricks on the back of the head. I remembered him mumbling something about his Uncle Han, who worked for the railroad out west in Hershey, Nebraska, where my dad grew up.

He said, "Uncle Han can drink five six-packs at a time without even coming up for air." Back then, we didn't pay much attention to his ramblings. But now, like a detective, I began to put it all together. Yep. Our father must have the gene too. All the more reason I should pursue a Master's degree in Psychiatric Nursing at Yale. I would be the one to fix my crazy family and save my father from his Beefeater's Gin, so he would not have to die a shameful death like my Uncle Junie. I would be the one to put the "fun" back into my "dysfunctional family."

They threw an enormous surprise party for me at work when I left to go to my Ivy League dream school. I sported a progressive bumper sticker on my car: "Uppity Women Unite." They gave me a card addressed to "Our Favorite Uppity Woman" and gifts galore. Everyone congratulated me on the achievement of getting into Yale. I left that job in a blaze of glory riding on chariots of fire. Even coworkers who previously kept their distance, like Roy, gave me cards and wished me well. I felt favored by the gods that day and full of joy. I cried at the party because their kindness touched my heart so much.

Pisswinks said, "I hate that bumper sticker and consider it divisive. It rubs me the wrong way." The man reeked of alpha male one-upmanship. He also confidentially told me, "I think my double standards on male and female higher education are perfectly okay and acceptable."

His big bosomed Italian mother represented his idea of the perfect female companion. A career housewife, she produced six children and stayed barefoot and pregnant for most of her married life with his doctor dad. This ideal fell very far from what I envisioned for my life and made it easy to leave Pisswinks behind.

My mother took me on a shopping spree and bought me a

black interview suit for Yale. I looked professional and spiffy that day, sliding my feet into new black patent leather Ferragamo pumps and shimming into a black tailored Liz Claiborne suit with three-quarter length sleeves and a white Liz Wear blouse. At thirty-eight, I felt proud I still possessed my girlish figure and fit into a size eight.

Mom made it clear she favored my entry into Yale. Being the first in her family to obtain a college degree, she favored higher education for women. An "uppity woman" in her way, she often reminded my father of her role in the family household as that of a "domestic engineer" rather than an ordinary housewife.

"A domestic engineer has to be able to run the household and is on the same level as any other type of engineer. Way above the role of a commonplace mediocre housewife who just does cooking and laundry. They could train a monkey to do the work of an ordinary housewife but you need the minimum of a college education to hold the title of domestic engineer, " she often said.   71

My father never argued with her but retorted by pouring himself another glass of Gin. He knew mother wore the pants in our family but deep down he loved her with all his heart and soul and wanted her to feel good about herself.

She continued to call him "the love of her life" even after fifty years of marriage. My friends called my parents "cute" because of their obvious devotion to each other. They still walked hand in hand and addressed one other as honey, dearest, and sweetheart. They lived in the same house, built in 1945 the year of my birth, for over fifty years. Pisswinks said he marveled at the stability of my family because his parents divorced several years ago and no longer lived together.

In early May of 1981, my parents drove me to Yale School of Nursing in New Haven, Connecticut where I met Judith Krauss, R.N., M.S.N., the director of the program, who later became my thesis advisor. Little did I know then, I would trudge through snowy gales and skid on black ice to visit her, turning in copy after copy of my thesis.

I cried the first time I saw the school. The brick walls of ivy I envisioned turned into reinforced concrete without an ivy leaf in sight. My dream institution lay in the middle of a combat zone. How disappointing. Close by the school, Yale New Haven Hospital's emergency room accepted their most common patients, trauma victims of gunshot and stab wounds and other crimes of violence.

But I put all negative thoughts aside on my interview day so my mind could focus. How excited I expected to feel, finally receiving a degree from an Ivy League school. I could picture how it would look on the wall, framed in gold. My family will be jumping for joy, with me floating on air.

That feeling of elation stayed with me all through the next three months. In September, I breezed through the stressful move into the dormitory, even though it took four trips back and forth between my parents' home and New Haven to finally feel comfortable. I brought everything but the proverbial kitchen sink with me, cramming it all into a tiny cubicle of two hundred and twenty-eight square feet they allotted for a single room.

After the breakup with Pisswinks, I felt vulnerable and alone as a single female of thirty-eight. Practically all the other students in my class lived with their spouses and families. Moving into the dormitory alone accentuated my single state all the more and made me feel sad.

Then, I learned from other students two students had been murdered near my dorm, leaving me feeling even more vulnerable and scared. I prayed to God to send me a friend to help me out in this loneliness crisis.

It didn't help to discover YSN recruited several militant gay feminists into its ranks and one of them appeared to be after me. In the library, the partner of Kristin flirted openly with me. I had earlier tried to befriend Kristin because she came from Massachusetts before I realized she appeared to be joined at the hip to another woman.

I responded with outrage to these flirtations to cover up sheer terror. I had never encountered this type of behavior before, although I read about it in books. YIKES. I didn't have a clue what to do except run and hide from her.

"I have to go," I said and ran out the library door, down the steps, and back to the safety of my lonely dorm room. My heart pounding in my ears, I sat staring out the window at the disappointing stark ivy-less walls and longed for the familiar peace and security of my parents' home in Lexington.

For the first time, I wondered if I had made a big mistake venturing into the big city and coming to Yale. They hadn't warned me about this weirdo behavior in the college catalog.

"You're pretty," Mike said, staring into my eyes the next day. I met him in the campus bookstore, standing in line to purchase books. We both realized we had chosen the same books and he told me he too belonged to the 1985 graduating class of Y.S.N.

Mike said, "I call Wyoming home, but for now, I too live in the dormitory." The only man in the program, he attracted attention due to his impressive six-foot-two stature. I needed a tall man to feel protected and less vulnerable and scared of the lesbian woman in the library and others like her. I viewed Mike as my ticket to the Ivy League degree I craved.

Even learning he belonged to the National Rifle Association and toted a firearm didn't matter. The incident in the library scared me to death, so I latched onto Mike like glue because I needed him for protection. Ironically, my new hero's last name happened to be Gay. Michael Gay would save me from the militant gay feminists who stood between me and that Ivy League diploma.

I started to walk back and forth to classes escorted by my new boyfriend, Kristin's girlfriend either saw or heard about us and left me alone. I never saw hide nor hair of her again. Although Mike's political and social views did not jibe with mine, but it didn't matter because I viewed him as helping me obtain my dream of a Yale degree.

"I graduated from the University of Montana Nursing program in Missoula, Montana and I carried my Glock 9 millimeter on my belt every day. I vote conservative and hate liberals, especially feminist liberals. A woman's place is in the home. I'm divorced, with no children. My wife lives back in Wyoming," he shocked me by announcing one day.

In his dorm room, he proudly showed me his firearm, complete with a holster and a patriotic flag. He stroked the trigger gently, kissing the smooth textured Teflon finish. I didn't dare reveal to him my negative feelings because I could tell he shared an important history with his Glock.

I told him nothing about Pisswinks but I did say, "I have never been married," causing his eyebrows to raise in surprise.

"I don't know any ladies over twenty-five who aren't married, most of them with at least a few kids. How come you haven't married yet?"

He posed this question to me suspiciously as if he expected me to confess to him my true bisexual nature or something.

"It takes time to obtain an education and I already have a master's degree from Tufts University in Massachusetts. I've focused on my education and career."

Nothing to hide, so why not tell him the truth? We came from two different worlds, which we knew from the beginning. They say opposites attract but in the case of Mike and me, I seriously doubted if we had any true attraction other than physical. He made it clear he found

78

me attractive but I felt repelled by his Glock, even frightened of it. I never had a boyfriend who carried a gun and I wasn't at all sure I felt comfortable about it. I buried my feelings because I still needed him to help me. He knew I needed him and he took every advantage of the situation.

The only man in the nursing program, Mike knew he would be in demand. Due to my naivety, I did not spot him as the opportunist he turned out to be.

During the middle of a harsh January winter, halfway through my first year, I ended up in the infirmary with a bad respiratory infection. My severe dust allergy contributed to the problem. They put me on intravenous antibiotics because I developed a cellulitis condition from blowing my nose so much. The cellulitis turned nasty and destroyed the skin cells of my nose. I had ugly red streaks all over my face and my nose started disintegrating right before my eyes.

"You could lose half your nose and need plastic surgery if we can't resolve this infection," the doctor at Yale New Haven Hospital said.

The stress of studying for all of the classes added to Mike's emotional distancing contributed to my illness. During my entire two months' stay in the hospital, he never visited me once. My parents stopped by to see me on their way to Florida and I cried tears of joy to see them.

"Oh, my God. They are telling me I could lose my nose! What will I do if I must have plastic surgery to rebuild my nose? What if they can't find the right antibiotic to put me on?" I confessed my deepest fears to them because I knew they loved me and I could trust them completely.

For some reason, my case stumped the Yale New Haven hospital physicians. They could not find the source of the infection to put me on the correct antibiotic. My father called the doctors to conference with them, while I lay in the hospital bed and tried to chat nonchalantly with my devoted mother about my studies.

"I am writing my thesis now. My thesis advisor is the same Judith Krauss you met, who is the director of the whole program. She is fabulous and understands I am down for the count with this disease but it will not affect my graduation from the program."

I reassured myself and Mother and prayed to God I would be able to graduate with my class despite this setback.

This occurred before the days of emails, so I received many phone calls from my thesis advisor wishing me well in the infirmary. My classmates supplied me with an entire collection of Stephen King novels.

They asked, " What are your favorite books?"

I answered, "Stephen King. I know his horror stories well

and need to bury myself in something to keep my mind off my current circumstances."

In time, the doctors found the right antibiotic to treat my condition and my cellulitis infection went away, leaving my nose perfect. I did not need plastic surgery. I left the infirmary knowing I could be sure of only my parents' loyalty and affection.

Mike ended up throwing me under the bus. He invited me to lunch at the local deli and broke the news saying, "When you got sick, I began to see someone else and we're heavily involved,"

"Bastard," I thought and watched him take a bite of his corned beef sandwich and kosher pickle and sip his diet coke. I said nothing to him. I needed his computer so I could type my thesis myself. Otherwise, I might have to pay someone to do it.

"Could I borrow your computer to type my thesis?" I

asked and munched my tuna melt sandwich. I knew he felt badly about cheating on me and I figured I'd take advantage of his guilty conscience to further my educational goals.

"I'll let you use it in my room, but you can't take it out of my room," he promised. So it happened Mike helped me in his way to secure my coveted Yale degree. In his dormitory room, I typed my thesis pecking away at the keys of his computer, turning in page after page to my two advisors for their approval.

During February, the coldest snowiest month that year, I trudged through snow-laden gales and skittered on black ice to hand deliver copies of my typed thesis to them. They corrected it manually and gave it back. I made the necessary revisions and returned with the revised edition. They liked my topic of "death anxiety" and complimented my research. This happened so many times I lost count.

I feared the deaths of both my parents deeply, my palms grew sweaty just contemplating it. I figured researching the topic of death, might help me lose my fear. I hoped to somehow be free of my fear by the time I reached my parents' age. My father just turned eighty-one, with my mother only a few years younger.

At age four, I climbed up on my father's knee saying, "Daddy, I'm afraid you're going to die," I fought back little girl tears.

"Oh, pumpkin, don't be afraid. That's not going to happen for a long time, " he reassured me.

We had just witnessed the untimely death of our dog Brownie due to a seizure. This misfortune triggered my first anxiety about the passing of loved ones in my family. This anxiety turned more intense as I grew older.

Dad already suffered from Arthritis pain in his right hip. I suspected this pain to be the reason behind his drinking because he never had an alcohol problem during our formative years. The doctors refused to perform the necessary hip replacement surgery due to cardiac issues. He already experienced two heart attacks along with an aortic aneurysm that nearly killed him five years ago. I figured he currently lived on borrowed time.

The thought of my father's death filled me with such intense anxiety, I couldn't bear to think about it. I knew I suffered from intense "death anxiety" and wrote my thesis about it.

They told us to pick a topic that grabbed our attention because otherwise, we would get bored with it. I felt driven by an obsession to find an answer to the mystery of my death anxiety. I searched to find a way out of my fear. This obsession pressed me to walk miles to see my thesis advisors and finish my project early, way before any of the others. I would graduate on time after all.

The thesis project turned into the most daunting task of

the YSN master's degree program, by far. The classwork, though challenging, came easily to me. I even passed the statistics class with flying colors. Cheryl had been right after all.

I somehow pushed through the other Herculean tasks of the program. In addition to the academic classes, we had clinical rotations. In my first year, I worked at the Connecticut Mental Health Center, or CMHC, doing assessments and evaluations of clients.

During my second year, I survived a tough placement in an all-female ward at the state hospital, Connecticut Valley Hospital in Middletown, Connecticut. This institution opened in 1868 and served as the public hospital for treating persons with mental illness. Ancient, mold-infested buildings and the stench of human excrement reminded me of a Gothic horror movie. I expected to see Boris Karloff walk out of there at any moment.

In this female unit, I met women incarcerated there for the majority of their adult lives, most confined there by their families at a time when women had few rights.

One lady I interviewed, who possessed especially poor social skills, held her head down to avoid eye contact with me during the entire hour-long interview.

"I don't want to talk," she mumbled, "Nothing to say."

Later, I sat in the only comfortable chair on the unit studying her chart and found her family had her committed due to an out-of-wedlock pregnancy. She had violated the social norms of her day, so they banished her from their sight. Reading further, I discovered the psychiatrist noted she'd been impregnated by a family member, so wore the shameful badge of being an incest victim.

"How awful," I murmured,"Now I understand why she can't make eye contact with anyone."

After this experience, I realized my gratitude for being born after this time when women had no rights and could be committed to mental hospitals by their families. Challenging as my circumstances seemed to be now, at least I lived at a time when families no longer exercised this kind of power over you just for being a woman.

On YSN graduation day, my parents finally met Mike. He split up with his girlfriend and told me he wanted us to get back together. The four of us had our photos taken,

That day is still a blur in my mind. I ended up graduating but Mike did not. He told me he deliberately dropped out of the program because it didn't agree with his politics.

"I'm going back to Wyoming where people understand me," Mike spoke bitterly. "They don't want to graduate me here for some reason."

Several of my friends did not graduate, including Millie, because she never turned in the final copy of her thesis.

Millie and I befriended one another as study buddies to help each other through the classes. Older than me by at least ten years, Millie commuted to the school from her home where she lived with her husband and family.

"I have a full life now, without a Yale degree," Millie told me on our first meeting.

"Then, why are you here?" I asked but she never answered.

I couldn't understand why no one else liked Millie. I couldn't see anything wrong with her, so I decided to trust her. Big mistake. She ended up doing me in and stabbing me in the back. Several other students warned me about her but I didn't recognize her true colors until too late.

Millie had a passive-aggressive personality. She smiled at you and said nice things to your face but said mean things about you behind your back. It turned out she resented me because studies came easily to me and I passed them all so well. She failed statistics and never understood what went on in her other classes either.

When it came time to graduate and decide the next step in my career, I made the mistake of trusting Millie. I knew I wanted to work for the Veteran's Administration Hospital in Bedford, Massachusetts, near our house in Lexington. She told me she knew an administrator there and had connections and would contact them to give me a reference.

"Trust me, sweetheart," Millie assured me with a wink of her eye, "I know just the right person to get you just the right job," she said and smiled demurely. This contact turned out to be responsible for one of the worst jobs I have ever had. I never saw any of it coming.

For deeply personal reasons, I wanted to work for the Veterans Administration. My favorite Uncle Junie served in the Army during World War Two. My Uncle Ray also served, captaining a Liberty ship carrying ammunition back and forth to the allies in the Pacific, a very dangerous mission. Because of the heroism of these two uncles, especially Uncle Junie, who left me funds for my nursing education, I felt a calling on my life to help veterans. I often wondered if a good psych nurse had been available to my Uncle Junie during those last years of his life, if he might not have had a different ending. I felt determined to try to see to it that no other soldier who had given so much of their lives to serve this nation would die in such sad and lonely circumstances. This is why it affected me so badly when the person Millie said could help me attain that position in the V. A. turned out to be such a disappointment.

After graduation, I moved back to my parent's home in Lexington. Mike and I split for good because we had nothing in common. At least I had my Yale degree. Even though I graduated with the YSN degree, qualifying me to work as a clinical nurse specialist, by the time I got to the V.A. hospital, they had eliminated this position. I got stuck working as a floor nurse and hated every minute of it. Millie's contact person had secured me this awful position. Working for the Bedford V.A. previously, I met a clinical nurse specialist who counseled patients with mental health issues. This was the job I wanted and this is what motivated me to obtain the YSN degree. What a disappointment when I learned they no longer employed nurses with these qualifications and the job had been eliminated.

The following winter of 1986, one year after my Yale graduation, Dad died suddenly in Florida of a heart attack following a bout with pneumonia. He told me the story over the phone. He volunteered for a White Sox baseball game in Sarasota Florida when a man deliberately coughed in his face, causing him to get sick. The cold turned into pneumonia and landed him in the hospital. I wanted to fly from Boston to Sarasota to see him but he told me, No.

"Dear, don't come now. I will get better from this and then you can come to visit."

But he never did get better. He died suddenly and I never got the chance to say goodbye. Here today and gone tomorrow. How strange this death thing is to take our loved ones away from us in a flash. How unfair and unjust.

They say time heals all wounds and wounds all heels. So true. At the memorial service, I read a dedication to my father, taken from a tape recording I had in his own words about his life growing up in Hershey, Nebraska. At the time, Pisswinks suggested I tape-record my father talking about his life.

'Thank you, Pisswinks. I love you," I whispered and read the words I took from the tape recording of my dad for his memorial service in our community church filled with his friends and family, including my mother, the love of his life, my brothers, and their families. What a priceless and treasured gift to give my dad, the best man I ever knew.

CHAPTER SEVEN
Honeymoon Phase

Between 2001 to 2005, I left hospital work and entered the field of home health. This transition alleviated the main problems of working in hospitals, including crazy coworkers and ineffective Administration. With home health, the nurse works alone with the patient. Your car becomes your office.

I worked for different companies in Hernando County. In 2015, I married my present husband, who lived in New Port Richey at that time, so I started a job with Encourage

Home Health, located only about twenty minutes from our home.

What impressed me the most about this company proved to be how easily they forgave employees who messed up and made mistakes. When first hired, I met a Licensed Practical Nurse with a huge shock of bushy red hair. I learned she had given the wrong medication to a patient. The primary care doctor in charge of this client removed all of his patients from the agency, which badly affected the corporate pocketbooks. Despite her error, this nurse did not lose her job. The supervisors treated her with courtesy and respect at the meetings we attended. I learned that Encourage Home Health supported their staff and treated them well.

Perhaps this was the reason I stayed with this company for almost six years. In the beginning, I worked as their only mental health R.N. but also saw medical patients.

Administration stood by me when I had the entire housekeeping staff at a local A.L.F. against me. The agency sent me there to administer an Insulin injection to a diabetic resident. At 6:45 A.M. I rang the bell at the facility so I would be in time to give the patient his 7:00 A.M. Insulin.

By the time, the staff answered the door, I found the client seated at the breakfast table in the dining room gobbling down scrambled eggs, bacon, and orange juice. The staff told me they didn't have the key to the medicine room and so I couldn't give him his Insulin. When I asked for the key, they said the head of the housekeeping department had it. I had to hunt her down, finally locating her on the third floor.

Irate at being bothered over the key, the housekeeping lady glared at me and curtly said, "Can't you see I am busy?"

"I'm sorry but the patient must have his Insulin because he's already eating his breakfast. I need the key now," I insisted.

She reluctantly handed the key over to me, all the while shooting me intense laser bullets of rage. She seemed determined to prove she would be calling the shots.

I returned by the elevator to the first-floor medication room, retrieved the Insulin, and administered the injection to the client. I left the facility with my stomach doing flip-flops because I had a sinking feeling the irate housekeeper would have the last word. The entire housekeeping staff lined up by the front door to glare at me when I tried to sneak out unnoticed. It seemed as if they felt the need to defend their turf against me, a foreign enemy invader.

By the time I arrived at Encourage thirty minutes later, I smelled trouble. All three supervisors attended a meeting behind the closed door of the Director of Nursing.

When they called me in to join them, my sweaty palms could barely hold my tablet and notebook. I told them my side of the story in a squeaky voice. As I had suspected, the A.L.F. housekeeping supervisor had already informed her boss of the incident. Her boss called our agency. By this time, my tears spilled out all over my scrubs. They handed me a Kleenex.

The Encourage administrator said, "Suzanne, they said you got rude and cursed at them. But, honestly, in all the time I have known you, I have never heard you swear, not even once."

Choking back the tears, I retorted, "I never swore at them."

I told them I suspected the resident was the one who cursed at them because he often yelled and screamed while using foul language when he didn't get his insulin shot on time.

In the end, they told me I could never return to that A.L.F. due to their complaints about me. That's fine with me, I thought, *"Good riddance to that facility with its crazy housekeeper and irate swearing patients. Good news for me because I never have to return there again."*

I never forgot how the Encourage Administration supported me through this nightmare. I had been warned by a coworker who did social work at another company to watch out for this administrator. She scared me to death but I never had a problem with her and she always gave me very good evaluations.

The administrator at Encourage ran a tight ship. Her daughter worked as a scheduler. I developed a good relationship with both of them and they called me often to see both medical and psychiatric patients. Under that regime, I fared well and earned plenty of money. This leadership lasted a good three or four years with a great stable office staff. I thrived in this new job and developed many close friendships with coworkers.

I like to call this my honeymoon phase in the Home Health Industry.

CHAPTER EIGHT
Changes

I turned left on a green arrow at the intersection of Trouble Creek and Rowan Road. Skies swirled gray with occasional patches of light blue. The radio played one of my favorite songs," One More Night" by Phil Collins. Smells of tuna fish permeated the air, having just purchased my favorite sub at Wawa. Clad in my purple scrubs, my mind jumped to thoughts of the patient I would see in seventeen minutes. He lived on Madison Avenue in a one-bedroom condo. My G.P.S. told me my exact arrival time right at his door.

When I entered the intersection, I saw the flash of a blue object hurtle in front of me. Like a lightning bolt, it came from nowhere. This ghost-like apparition hit me broadside at an accelerated speed. My head hit the windshield while my left wrist jammed into the steering wheel. It all happened so quickly, my racing thoughts turned to scrambled eggs. The tuna sub careened in all directions from the impact of the crash, creating a storm of fish and lettuce inside my car.

"Oh, my God. What do I do now?" "What if it's my fault? "My wrist must be broken because it hurts so much." Thoughts whirled around my head like a blender on steroids.

My head hurt too and I couldn't release my wrist from the steering wheel. Finally, I untangled my limp wrist but it didn't look normal. I knew it had to be broken.

"What if it's broken so I can't work anymore?" "What if it's my fault?"

This last horror gripped me over and over again. Panicked, I looked around to see if anyone had witnessed the accident.

I saw no one. Stepping on the gas, I drove my car out of the intersection and onto a nearby street. I thought I heard a police siren in the distance and got a clear vision of myself sitting in a jail cell.

"Are you crazy? You just left the scene of an accident! They will lock you up for this!" My whirling emotions spinning out of control, I drove down side streets looking for a hidimg place. Finally, I came to a mobile home park where I found a huge blue dumpster to camouflage my car.

I drove my car to the back of the park and breathed a sigh of relief for the first time. For two hours, I stayed hidden behind the dumpster, not daring to come out. I called my patient to reschedule the visit for another day. There I sat, behind the dumpster, wondering why this police paranoia plagued me so much. I figured all the speeding tickets in my youth must have negatively impacted my psyche.

After the police sirens abated, I drove out of the mobile home park. Palms sweating, heart fluttering out of control, I set the G.P.S. to go home. My car knew the way and drove me there swiftly. I had nothing to do with it.

"My God! What happened to your car?", my husband screamed when he saw the damage. For the first time, I surveyed my poor vehicle. The front bumper hung by a thread. Blue paint covered the crumpled-up hood which had collapsed, exposing the engine. It didn't look like a car anymore. My beautiful Ford Freestyle morphed into a worthless piece of junk.

"You're going to have to get a new one. This looks like at least $5000 worth of damage here." My husband broke the bad news to me and I started to cry.

"My wrist is broken, I'm sure." I showed him my limp left

appendage which I could not even move because of the pain. Chunks of tuna fish clung to my scrubs which I picked off and gobbled down. My stomach grumbled in hunger. The accident interfered with my lunch.

The rest of that day passed by quickly, filled with a visit to the emergency room, x-rays of my wrist, prescribed pain pills, and a splint on the wrist to stabilize the injury and alleviate the pain. It turned out to be broken but I still needed to work and drive despite my injury.

Throughout the rest of the day, I expected to see a police car pull up to the door to arrest me for leaving the scene of an accident. The nagging fear it had been my fault remained with me. What had I done except turn left on a green arrow?

When I reviewed it all with my husband, he told me I did nothing wrong.

"The other driver must have run the red light at the intersection. You turned left on a green arrow and he should have stopped. He caused a T-bone accident," he said to comfort me.

I continued to fear the police would find me and I would end up in jail. This dread stayed with me and haunted me for months after the accident. The terror still grips me now every time I get behind the wheel of a car.

I had nightmares about the accident. This became the main reason I wanted to leave home health and why I took a class to be certified to teach English as a Second Language.

In August 2021, the Covid 19 Pandemic hit. I took my ESL certification class via Zoom because they canceled all in-person classes.

In my role as a front-line "essential worker" mental health R.N. with Encourage Home Health, I became busier than ever. I acquired a small caseload of fear-stricken clients, mostly women, who suffered from "Agoraphobia" or "fear of the marketplace." "Agora' is a word derived from the ancient Greek meaning "marketplace."

Before this, the entire office staff changed. The Administrator and her daughter returned to New England. They told me she felt homesick for the autumn leaves and seasonal changes.

With Covid came Zoom case conference meetings, so we no longer had weekly in-person meetings. So many new people joined all at once, I gave up on remembering their names.

The car wreck in 2018 traumatized me to the core. I ended up buying a practically brand-new Ford Explorer. I took extra precautions at intersections, looking both ways before daring to go out. I set limits with the agency and told them I would only see patients in West Pasco and would no longer drive into East Pasco. They were fine with it.

After this, a curious thing occurred. I began to see another side to my "desire to retire" dilemma. I experienced two surgeries for other issues. My Encourage family provided me with love and support through these traumatic episodes, causing me to see the positive side of my nursing job.

During the summer of 2020, I chose to have an elective right knee replacement surgery. This meant a three-month hiatus from Encourage Home Health and a welcome break from driving. My O.T. coworker friend proved to be invaluable during this time. She advised me about everything from showering safely to choosing the proper walker and cane. My physical therapist coworker provided important information to help me recover. She told me about exercises I could practice to develop strength. She suggested I work out daily on a stationary bike to improve the motion in my right knee. This exercise bike helped me the most to get back on my feet again.

Then in May of 2021, I had another right leg surgery on my Femur. After an unexpected fall, I developed a hairline fracture in the largest and longest bone in my body. This surgery resulted in another three-month absence from work and driving. Again, Encourage treated me with kindness and support. They visited me with floral bouquets, sympathy cards, and empathetic phone messages flooding in weekly.

After this break from driving, my flashbacks to the 2018 car accident began to subside. I obsessed less about the police being after me and my sleep became less troubled by nightmares. I grew more confident that I might drive again and put this negative experience behind me for good.

I realized I did not wish to retire from Encourage. I don't know what I would have done without my coworkers standing by me during these crises in my life. Their positive energy helped me recover, both emotionally and physically. I refused to have a pity party during this time and decided to feel grateful for being blessed with such caring people in my life. Why would I want to retire from a company with such encouraging, supportive coworkers?

CHAPTER NINE
Reality Shock

Causes of Reality Shock

- Culture shock
  - Work culture is different and unfamiliar
  - Providing "wholistic care" may not be reality
- Methods of evaluation
  - Work world evaluates on quantity of care
  - Academic world evaluates on correct steps
- Incongruent school and work values

Mosby items and derived items

So, there you have my story. I now feel ambivalent about the idea of retirement from Encourage Home Health. Though nursing was never my dream job, the positives outweighed the negatives in terms of my position with Encourage as a psych nurse.

Every time I get the urge to quit Encourage, something else occurs to keep me staying on. The big thing now is money and the fact is this job pays the bills. I cannot seem to retain enough ESL students at one time because they keep quitting. Most of my online ESL students have gone by the wayside. Perhaps the reason for this is that they are teenagers and nothing ever remains stable in the life of an adolescent. My goal is to find more long-term adult ESL students.

I currently have a thirty-five-year-old Puerto Rican fellow coming to the house one evening per week. He faithfully pays me cash for each hourly lesson. He has a wife and two children in Puerto Rico and he told me they plan to come to America at the end of October.

I have several suggestions for people wanting to change careers, based on my own experiences. You need to keep doing both occupations for a while until you start making money at your dream job. This could take a long while so it is very easy to become discouraged. You need to do whatever you can do during this time to keep the faith that you will eventually succeed at what you believe in. Don't give up!

Setting boundaries at my regular nursing job helped me also. Think about what it is about the regular job you don't like and then set limits with your company. For me, it was all the driving so restricting my territory to West Pasco helped to put me more in control, setting the necessary boundaries I needed. I realized dealing with too much traffic put me over the edge. By setting this rule with the company, I bettered my situation greatly.

A sit-down talk with your immediate supervisor might be necessary to set the limits you will need to make your job tolerable while you wait for your dream job to take off. If you have been in your present position for a long while, Administration will not want to lose you. They would rather work with you to improve your situation to keep you on board.

Above all, try your best to keep a positive attitude with a smile on your face. You will have better luck making improvements at your regular job with a pleasant attitude than if you show up to work in a disgruntled, ugly mood. You want to be in control and walk out of that job by choice and not get fired due to your rotten attitude.

It is normal to go from a "honeymoon phase" to "reality shock" in any job, just as it is in a marriage. In the beginning, everything seems fantastic but, later, your rose-colored glasses start to fade and you see the flaws you failed to notice in the beginning. Understand this and know there is no perfect job, just as there is no perfect mate. You will need to weather this storm and make up your mind to stay on your job until you no longer need the money it provides. This is only realistic.

For me, finding trustworthy coworkers to whom I could verbalize my wrath when feeling frustrated, helped me keep on working, even when I felt upset with Administration. Talking to my friends who had experienced similar problems helped and kept me from quitting. I also developed the practice of writing emails instead of picking up the phone to deliver angry messages. An email is more impersonal than a text message or a phone call and so, is usually received better by the recipient.

Above all, you must not give up and believe you will succeed. If you are good at what you do and put the work into it, your efforts are bound to pay off in the end. You will finally succeed at your dream job. This may take some ingenuity on your part, a change in marketing and or advertising. For me, Google has made a huge difference because students who are using Google to find ESL instructors will find my name at the top of the list. My website creator set me up with Google and this has helped a lot. The majority of the phone calls I receive are from people who found me on Google.

I wish you the best of luck in your dream career.. Please remember there is no such thing as failure. Your breakthrough could be right around the corner! NEVER GIVE UP!

CHAPTER TEN
The Party

"The more you praise and celebrate your life, the more there is in life to celebrate" Oprah Winfrey

Debbie, my retired occupational therapist friend, called to tell me something important. This happened after I turned in my computer and finally called it quits with my nursing job.

"You and I need to have a retirement party. Even though this administration is negative and unsupportive, we still have coworkers who love us and miss us. We need to end this job on a positive note."

After working nearly eight years with the company, I had to agree.

"My feelings are so hurt they never acknowledged my leaving," I confided to her forlornly. I remembered the huge celebration my coworkers gave me on the psych unit in Massachusetts when I left for Yale. I looked back on my "honeymoon phase" with this company and missed those days. "Reality shock" felt painful and depressing. How could they treat me so unfairly and not acknowledge my retirement when I worked for them for so long?

"It's not like it used to be. Companies don't throw retirement shindigs anymore. It's nothing against you. You know this Administration stinks for their lack of support. Don't take it personally. I worked for them even longer than you did and they never recognized my retirement either."

I knew Debbie made sense and it made me feel better when I realized I didn't have to take this lack of recognition personally. We both agreed the former Administration would have treated us with more respect and would have acknowledged our leaving.

116

So we planned our own retirement party together. We chose ten coworkers to invite to my house for a cookout in October. These people included physical therapists, physical therapy assistants, nurses, occupational therapists, and their significant others. Debbie offered to bring hotdogs and hamburgers and I agreed to provide the retirement cake and the wine.

Due to the extra workload from the company, everyone begged for the celebration to take place on a Saturday and not a working night. No problem. We scheduled it for October 28th, after she made a phone call to Cynthia, who suggested the date. Cynthia is the physical therapist who helped me so much after my Femur surgery.

"Cindy, You are amazing. You helped me walk again. How can I thank you enough," I praised her for all the hard work she invested in my recovery. I still do the exercises she gave me.

We agreed on one rule. No politics. I knew we all had different viewpoints. I didn't want any arguments to spoil it. Debbie and Cynthia agreed to spread the word to the others about the date, time, and place.

I ordered a sheet cake from Publix with the words: "Happy Retirement": a carrot cake with yummy thick white frosting.

"Scrumptious," said Patty, tasting the cake for the first time.

My husband cooked on the grill and it all turned out delicious. I served my blueberry and cranberry wine to those who requested it. Others brought their own beer and alcoholic beverages. In the end, the whole affair cost me very little.

Our handyman friend Nick, hooked up my laptop to play music and we laughed and sang and danced a little under the trees in my backyard. It felt like a good way to close an important chapter in my life. Having a little fun with some of the most dedicated talented healthcare workers I have known over the years.

Looking back on this party, Debbie and I both concluded our time at Encourage as time well invested. We helped a lot of people, and acquired friends we would keep for the rest of our lives.

In some ways, it helped me to better understand my dad and

how he felt when he retired, after spending his life in one field. But, unlike my dad, I have chosen to fill my life with other worthwhile things, especially my writing. The relationships I formed with other local authors through our writer's group have filled my life with purpose and meaning, empowering me to peel back the layers of myself and discover the best and worst parts. I can work on the worst parts and nurture the best parts and look forward to celebrating many years of a fulfilling life.

The fun of this party offset the negative and brought me closure. The emotional scars from the past didn't pain me any longer.   All is well.

ABOUT THE AUTHOR

Suzanne A. Ries is a well-educated, well-traveled woman who lives with her husband in the Tampa Bay area of Florida. She has a good deal of experience in life, having lived in Alaska, Boston, and Florida, and has traveled to several countries. She holds two Master's Degrees from top Ivy League universities and is also professionally certified to teach English as a second language

.

Having authored two books besides this one, she is currently working on publishing an anthology of her original poems and essays which will be out soon. Suzanne is a woman of many talents and interests and wears many hats. She is an Amway representative, a published author, a motivational speaker, a registered nurse, an accomplished amateur photographer, a knowledgeable, adventuresome health chef, and an active environmentalist. Her philanthropic efforts include providing financial support for a child in the Philippines and sending help to several animal rescue missions. She also partners with Joyce Meyer Ministries.

Suzanne believes it is never too late to make changes in your life and a person is never too old to go on adventures or enjoy the good things in life. Her website is https://keyesl.us

You can contact Suzanne at: suzanneabbo1@gmail.com

Suzanne after graduating from Newton Wellesley Hospital School of Nursing in Newton Massachusetts for Registered Nurse education.

Suzanne today

THE   **END!**

Made in the USA
Coppell, TX
28 November 2023

24879175R00075